LET'S LOOK AT
CASTLES

Rupert Matthews

Reading Consultant
Diana Bentley
University of Reading

Artist
John James

The Bookwright Press
New York · 1988

Let's Look At

First published in the
United States in 1988 by
The Bookwright Press
387 Park Avenue South
New York, NY 10016

First published in 1988 by
Wayland (Publishers) Ltd
61 Western Road, Hove
East Sussex BN3 1JD, England

Library of Congress Catalog Card Number: 87–73384

ISBN 0–531–18204–5

Phototypeset by Kalligraphics Ltd, Redhill, Surrey
Printed by Casterman, S.A., Belgium

Words printed in
bold are explained
in the glossary

Contents

The first castles

Two thousands years ago people in Britain lived in groups called tribes. Each tribe had a hilltop fortress to protect it from enemies. These hill forts were surrounded by deep ditches. The houses in the hill fort were made of wood.

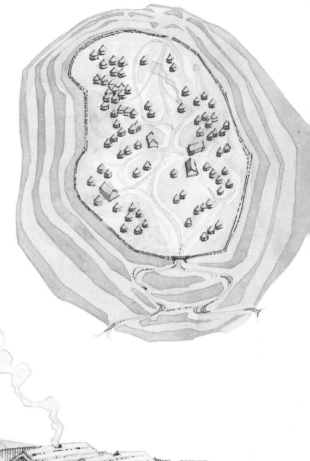

One thousand years ago a new type of castle appeared. It had a large enclosure in which the people lived, called the bailey. Beside this was a mound of earth with a tower on top. This was called the motte, so these castles are called motte and bailey castles. If the castle was attacked, the people retreated to the motte.

The castle in peacetime

Castles were built with thick walls in case they were attacked, but most of the time there was no war. The people who lived in castles were able to live normal, peaceful lives.

The lord and lady of the castle lived in the comfortable rooms that were built inside. Many soldiers and servants lived in the castle too. Each person who lived in the castle had a job to do. Can you see what these people are doing?

Lords and knights

Lords and knights who lived in castles needed to be very good at fighting. If a war began, the lords and knights would have to go to fight. They spent many hours practicing with weapons such as swords, **lances** and axes.

Young men who wanted to become knights also had to train with weapons. They were called **squires**.
When they were not training, knights often rode horses to go hunting or **hawking**. Sometimes ladies went riding with the knights.

Cochem Castle, Germany

Parts of a castle

Each part of the castle was important. The bailey was an open area in which people could work and trade. Soldiers who were on duty stayed in the **guardroom** or walked along the **parapet**. Prisoners were kept in the **dungeons**. In the Great Hall everyone in the castle would gather for feasts and important occasions.

11

Markets and castles

Markets were often held at castles. Farmers and craftsmen from the nearby countryside came to the markets to sell their goods. Sometimes merchants from distant countries came to sell strange goods. Markets were exciting events. People could meet to talk and have fun.

Krak des Chevaliers, Syria

13

Eating and drinking

Everybody in a castle ate together in the Great Hall. Knights, **clergymen** and other important people sat near the lord and lady of the castle. Less important people sat at the other end of the room. There were no forks or spoons, so everybody ate with their fingers. Sometimes they used knives to cut up pieces of meat. Favorite meals were stews and roast chicken. Potatoes had not yet been discovered, so people ate bread with their meal.

Sometimes a **minstrel** would sing songs to keep people amused.

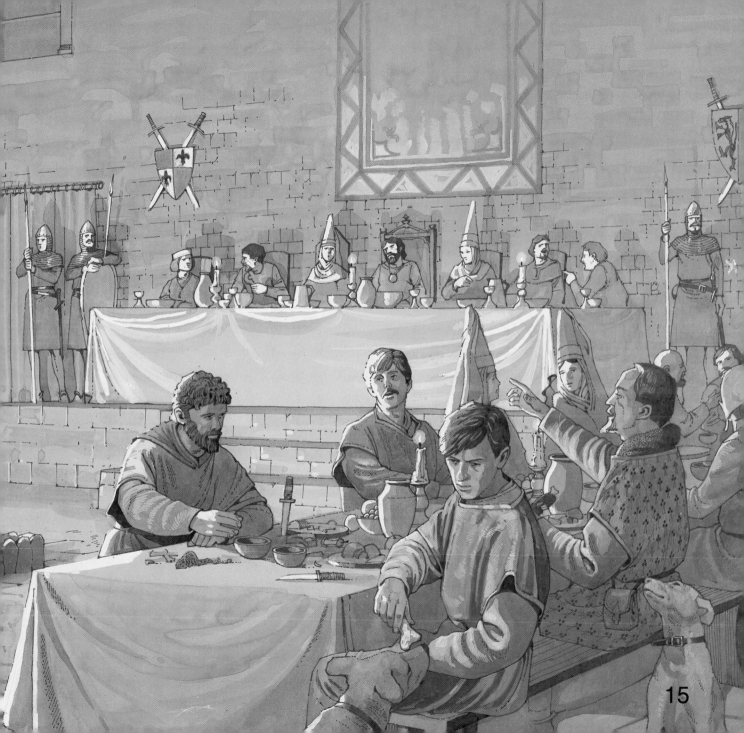

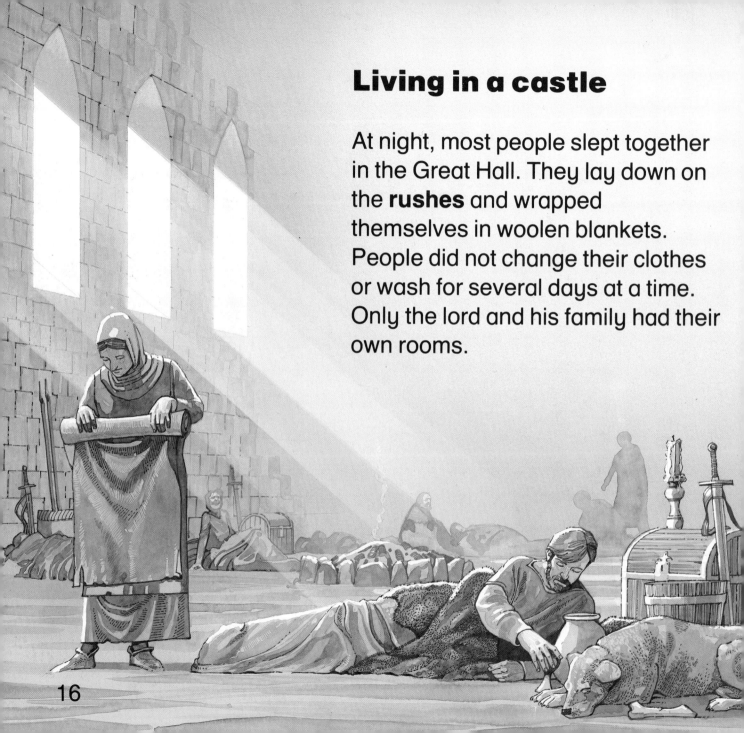

Living in a castle

At night, most people slept together in the Great Hall. They lay down on the **rushes** and wrapped themselves in woolen blankets. People did not change their clothes or wash for several days at a time. Only the lord and his family had their own rooms.

Castles were cold and drafty places.
Large fires were kept burning in
nearly every room to keep people
warm. To stop the drafts, thick
tapestries were hung over the
doorways. Everyone wore thick
clothes made of wool or fur.

Entertainment

Sometimes the lord of the castle would organize a great event for everyone in the castle.

A favorite entertainment was a tournament. All the knights and lords in the area would come to the castle. They would fight each other with blunt weapons to prove who was the best knight.

Caernarvon Castle, Wales

A visit from the king

Years ago kings and queens often traveled throughout their lands visiting important people. When the lord of a castle heard that the king was coming, he tried to make the castle look as grand as possible. The castle would be cleaned and the **battlements** hung with **banners**. The lord and all his servants would wear their very best clothes. Expensive foods would be served to the king.

Bodiam Castle, England

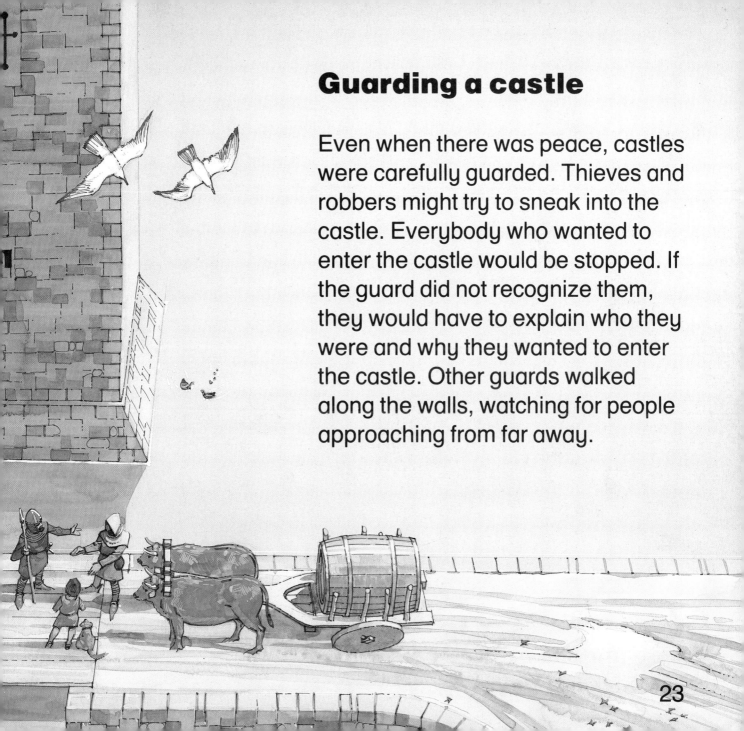

Guarding a castle

Even when there was peace, castles were carefully guarded. Thieves and robbers might try to sneak into the castle. Everybody who wanted to enter the castle would be stopped. If the guard did not recognize them, they would have to explain who they were and why they wanted to enter the castle. Other guards walked along the walls, watching for people approaching from far away.

The castle under attack

Sometimes a castle would come under attack by enemy armies. The attackers needed to break into the castle in order to capture it. They would build machines of war to try to batter down the walls. These included **battering rams, catapults** and **belfries**. Sometimes they even tried to dig a tunnel into the castle.

The defenders fought back with bows and arrows and boiling water. At night they would sometimes rush out of the castle and try to destroy the attackers' machines.

The decline of the castle

Six hundred years ago, people began to leave the castles. There were several reasons for this. The new cannons could batter a hole in a castle in just a few hours. Castles were no longer safe against large armies.

There were also fewer bands of robbers and thieves. This meant that the lords no longer needed to live in uncomfortable castles. Many lords built grand new houses and moved out of their castles. By the year 1500, castles were old-fashioned.

Caerlaverock Castle, Scotland

Castles today

Over the years many castles have become ruins. Some castles, however, are still the homes of lords or rich people. Many of these castles are open to the public. You can wander through the stone halls and walk along the walls or even climb towers. If you go abroad and visit one of these castles, try to imagine what it must have been like long ago. Just think how many people have also walked along the corridors.

The main hall, Arundel Castle, England

Glossary

Banners   Brightly colored flags, often very long and beautifully decorated.

Battering ram   A long wooden beam that was swung at castle walls to knock them down.

Battlements   Low walls on top of the main castle walls. Soldiers could shelter behind them when under attack.

Belfry   A large tower made of wood. It was filled with knights and soldiers and pushed against the walls of a castle. The soldiers would then climb out onto the castle walls.

Catapult   A machine that hurled large stones. It was used to attack a castle.

Clergyman   A member of the church, such as a priest, bishop or monk.

Dungeons   Small dark rooms where prisoners were kept, usually underground.

Guardroom   A room, usually close to the gate of a castle, for the guards to use.

Hawking   Hawks are large birds that kill other animals for food. For this sport they were sent to catch wild birds, such as pigeons.

Lances   Long spears.

Minstrel   A singer and storyteller who entertained knights and lords during feasts.

Parapet   The walkway along the top of a castle wall.

Rushes   Long grass that was dried and put on floors.

Squire   A young man, usually the son of a knight or lord, who was training to become a knight.

Tapestries   Decorated wall hangings, usually made of woolen cloth.

Books to read

Castles, by Beth Smith. Franklin Watts, 1988.

Castles of the Middle Ages, by Pierre Miquel. Silver, 1985.

Learning About Castles and Palaces by Ruth S. Odor. Children's Press, 1982.

Living in Castle Times, by Robyn Gee, ed. EDC Publishers, 1982.

See Inside a Castle, rev. edition by R.J. Unstead. Franklin Watts, 1986.

Index